FOCUS ON MEDIA BIAS

# BIAS IN REPORTING ON CLIMATE CHANGE

by Connor Stratton

FOCUS
READERS.

VOYAGER

# www.focusreaders.com

Focus Readers is distributed by North Star Editions:
sales@northstareditions.com | 888-417-0195

Produced for Focus Readers by Red Line Editorial.

Photographs ©: Shutterstock Images, cover, 1, 8–9, 14–15, 17, 21, 22, 29, 31, 32–33, 35, 40–41, 43, 44; Julio Cortez/AP Images, 4–5, 39; Olivier Douliery/AP Images, 7; Dennis Cook/AP Images, 11; Red Line Editorial, 13, 27; Richard Drew/AP Images, 18–19; Alberto E. Tamargo/Sipa USA/AP Images, 24–25; Dar Yasin/AP Images, 37

**Library of Congress Cataloging-in-Publication Data**
Names: Stratton, Connor, author.
Title: Bias in reporting on climate change / by Connor Stratton.
Description: Lake Elmo, MN : Focus Readers, [2022] | Series: Focus on media bias | Includes
   bibliographical references and index. | Audience: Grades 4-6
Identifiers: LCCN 2021000746 (print) | LCCN 2021000747 (ebook) | ISBN 9781644938621 (hardcover) |
   ISBN 9781644939086 (paperback) | ISBN 9781644939543 (ebook) | ISBN 9781644939949 (pdf)
Subjects: LCSH: Climatic changes in mass media--Juvenile literature. | Climatic changes--Press coverage--
   United States--Juvenile literature. | Mass media--Objectivity--United States--Juvenile literature.
Classification: LCC P96.C582 S77 2022  (print) | LCC P96.C582  (ebook) | DDC 363.738/74--dc23
LC record available at https://lccn.loc.gov/2021000746
LC ebook record available at https://lccn.loc.gov/2021000747

Printed in the United States of America
Mankato, MN
082021

# ABOUT THE AUTHOR

Connor Stratton writes and edits nonfiction children's books. When he was born, the amount of carbon dioxide in the atmosphere was 356 parts per million. As of 2021, it was 415 parts per million.

# TABLE OF CONTENTS

# CHAPTER 1

# NOT UP FOR DEBATE

On September 29, 2020, Fox News hosted a presidential debate. The event featured Donald Trump and Joe Biden. They were the two main candidates for US president. More than 70 million people watched. US citizens would soon vote for president. It was a rare chance for voters to see both candidates together.

Presidential debates often have little effect on an election. However, debates can show how the

**During a 2020 debate, President Donald Trump minimized the role that humans play in causing climate change.**

media frames issues. Hosts ask questions that they believe voters care about. For example, Chris Wallace of Fox News asked both candidates about **climate change**. It was significant that Wallace mentioned the topic at all. A debate host hadn't brought up climate change in 20 years. Wallace's questions showed how much people cared about the problem in 2020.

Even so, some climate experts criticized Wallace for how he framed the issue. Wallace asked President Trump what he believed about climate change science. He also asked if Trump believed humans were causing climate change. These questions made it seem like climate science was up for debate.

In fact, the vast majority of scientists agree that humans have been causing climate change. They also agree that climate change is a serious

▲ Many climate experts said moderator Chris Wallace failed to stress the scientific consensus about climate change.

problem. But many Americans do not know these facts about climate change. The US media is part of the reason why. Media **bias** about climate change has been widespread for decades. As a result, it can be difficult for people to learn about the issue.

# CHAPTER 2

# HISTORY OF CLIMATE CHANGE COVERAGE

Human-caused climate change began in the 1800s. That was when the **Industrial Revolution** spread to many countries around the world. People started using huge amounts of fossil fuels for energy. Fossil fuels include coal, oil, and natural gas.

Scientists first understood the **greenhouse effect** in the 1890s. During the mid-1900s, scientists connected the greenhouse effect to

**During the Industrial Revolution, people started using fossil fuels to power factories.**

human action. Burning fossil fuels was putting massive amounts of carbon gases into the air. These gases were causing global warming.

By the 1980s, scientists had reached widespread agreement about human-caused climate change. Scientists also agreed that the problem required action. Government leaders started discussing climate change. Fossil fuel companies did, too. Even so, news outlets rarely reported on the topic.

In 1988, that started to change. A scientist told the US Congress that humans were causing climate change. In addition, the summer of 1988 was the hottest in memory. News about climate change surged in response. Articles in 1988 and 1989 largely matched the science.

However, climate change coverage soon shifted. **Conservative** leaders and fossil fuel

In the late 1980s, Dr. James Hansen warned the US Senate about the dangers of climate change.

companies helped cause this shift. Conservative leaders believed governments should not control the economy. But governments would need greater control to slow climate change. So, conservative leaders opposed taking action.

Fossil fuel companies knew their products were causing climate change. However, slowing climate change would require people to decrease their use of fossil fuels. The companies opposed this action. They wanted to keep their profits high.

Fossil fuel companies worked with conservative leaders. Together, they helped cast doubt on climate change. They also supported the small number of scientists who denied climate change. Through the 1990s, news media included these doubtful voices. To many people, climate science started to appear uncertain. This uncertainty made it easier for governments to avoid action.

The trend continued during the 2000s. Climate change deniers gained positions in the US government. These leaders prevented climate action. Conservative media also featured climate change deniers. As a result, many conservatives remained unsure about climate change. In contrast, **progressives** tended to believe climate science. People in the center did, too.

In the 2010s, many people began getting their news from social media sites. These sites often spread false ideas about climate change. But some social media users took climate change seriously. For example, millions of young people started protesting in favor of climate action. They used social media to bring attention to their protests.

# CLIMATE VIEWS BY POLITICAL PARTY ◁

This graph shows the percentage of Americans who believe that the effects of climate change have already started.

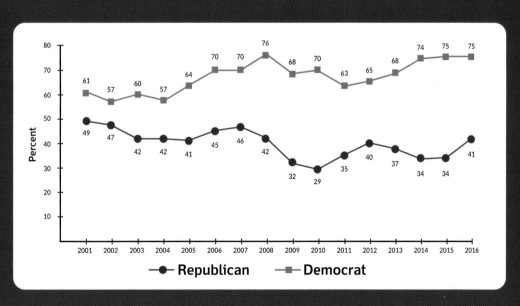

# CHAPTER 3

# IGNORING THE PROBLEM

News media help people learn about current events. Media also help people decide what matters. If news sources do not report on a subject, people are less likely to learn about it. People are even less likely to believe the subject is important.

Climate change is one of these subjects. As climate coverage increases, public interest in the topic increases, too. News coverage can also

**News media help voters understand which lawmakers support action on stopping climate change.**

influence who people vote for. This is significant because lawmakers have the power to address the climate crisis.

Since the 1990s, climate change has received increasing news attention. However, many climate activists believe the amount of coverage is still not enough. In 2018, the four largest US television networks spent a combined total of 142 minutes discussing climate change on their news shows. In 2019, that number increased to 238 minutes. Even so, climate change made up less than 1 percent of the networks' news coverage in 2019.

Climate change doesn't get much attention on local TV either. In 2017, only one-third of weather

## ➤ THINK ABOUT IT

Which news topics do you see most often? Which topics do you think should be covered more? Why?

▲ Climate change can lead to strong storms, which can lead to more flooding.

reporters mentioned climate change on TV. Many media experts believe that number needs to be much higher. If climate change is not mentioned, viewers may not realize the issue affects them.

Newspapers tend to cover climate change more often than TV networks. And in 2019, major US newspapers covered the topic much more than they had in previous years. However, many people don't read newspapers. In 2019, nearly half of Americans saw climate change news less than once a month.

# CHAPTER 4

# FACTS AND ACCURACY

news media often explain climate science incorrectly. For example, some articles argue that climate change is not happening at all. Others claim that humans are not causing climate change. And some state that climate change is not serious. But these views are not supported by the vast majority of climate experts.

False claims often depend on fallacies. In a fallacy, people use flawed reasoning to support an

**In the first six months of 2019, Fox News host Tucker Carlson ran 41 segments that rejected climate science.**

argument. Many fallacies involve cherry-picking. When people cherry-pick, they focus on only the information that supports their claim. They ignore the other data.

In 2020, a popular article relied heavily on cherry-picking. The author argued that climate change was not a serious problem. To make his case, he challenged the idea that climate change was making extreme weather more common.

The author cherry-picked a number of facts for this argument. For example, he stated that the number of fires around the world has decreased. This fact was true. However, the author's source

In 2020, California set a new record for the number of acres burned in wildfires.

was referring to fires set by humans. The author used a fact about human-set fires to make an argument about wildfires. He also ignored the data showing how climate change has made wildfires much worse.

Even when reporters accept climate science as fact, they do not always present the science accurately. In 2018, a United Nations group published a report. It stated that fossil fuel usage had to be cut nearly in half from 2010 levels

In a 2018 report, the United Nations called for a huge decrease in the number of coal-fired power stations.

by 2030. Otherwise, Earth's average temperature would rise too much. It would become 2.7 degrees Fahrenheit (1.5°C) higher than it was before the Industrial Revolution. Scientists believe the most serious effects of climate change will happen if this increase in temperature occurs.

The 2018 report received heavy media attention. Climate experts hoped this attention would lead to greater action. But they also worried about how the media framed the report. Much of the reporting focused on the 2030 deadline. Some reports even claimed people had until 2030 to save the world.

The science was more complex. The report did say that human actions before 2030 were important. Those actions could prevent the worst effects of climate change. But actions after 2030 still mattered.

Some climate experts believed the focus on 2030 could stop people from acting. Solving the climate crisis requires massive changes. Faced with such big changes, many people feel helpless. Focusing on the short deadline could make more people give up on the issue.

# CHAPTER 5

# REPORTING "BOTH SIDES"

News reporters have certain rules they try to follow. One main rule is to be balanced. Balanced reporting shows all sides of an issue. For many topics, this approach makes sense. Reporters try not to take sides in politics, for example. They explain what all major political parties believe. If a reporter discussed only one party's views, the reporter could appear to be biased.

**Reporters attempt to maintain balance when reporting on politics, but this strategy can have harmful effects when reporting on climate change.**

Balanced reporting can make it seem like both sides are equally supported. For US politics, this split is largely true. But some topics are not equally split. For these topics, balanced reporting can make one side seem much more credible than it actually is.

Researchers studied articles about climate change from the 1990s. Most articles gave half their space to scientists. The other half went to climate change deniers. These voices denied that humans were causing climate change. This balance would make sense if scientists were equally divided. But approximately 97 percent of climate scientists agree that humans are causing climate change. By giving equal space to deniers, news articles told a false story. They made it seem like the two sides had equal support. As a result, some readers believed the science was unclear.

In the 2000s, major US newspapers started giving less space to climate change deniers. By the early 2010s, deniers got even less space. But conservative papers continued to feature deniers.

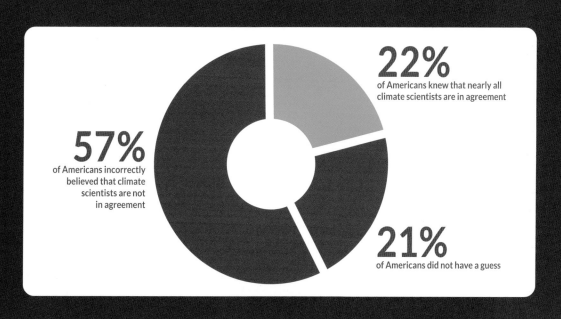

# CLIMATE CONFUSION ◄

Approximately 97 percent of climate scientists agree that humans are causing climate change. But according to a 2019 survey, most Americans didn't know this fact.

**22%**
of Americans knew that nearly all climate scientists are in agreement

**57%**
of Americans incorrectly believed that climate scientists are not in agreement

**21%**
of Americans did not have a guess

False balance remained common in other media. Many TV networks gave equal time to scientists and climate change deniers. Meanwhile, conservative TV networks largely treated climate change as an unclear issue.

In the 2010s and early 2020s, some media experts believed the false-balance problem was changing. Major newspapers still gave lots of space to people who opposed taking action on climate change. These voices often admitted that humans were causing climate change. However, they argued against taking action to solve the problem.

## ➤ THINK ABOUT IT

Balanced reporting often treats an issue as if it has only two sides. How many sides do you believe climate change has? Which ones seem the most important to you?

▲ The rise of social media in the 2000s made it easier for climate change deniers to spread false information.

Business groups often made up these voices. They received more media attention than many other groups. In fact, scientists often received the least attention from the media. As a result, many readers and viewers got the impression that climate action was not necessary or important. This doesn't reflect the position of scientists, who call for immediate and massive changes.

# SKEPTICAL SCIENCE

Skepticism is a key part of science. Scientists don't say they are sure about an idea unless they have strong evidence. Skepticism encourages new ideas about the world. It also encourages scientists to gather more evidence for existing ideas.

For instance, some scientists had ideas about global warming in the early 1900s. At least one scientist believed fossil fuels were warming the planet. At the time, other scientists were not sure. This skepticism was useful. After all, Earth's climate is very complex. There was not yet enough information.

Early doubts helped raise important questions about climate change. Scientists did research to answer those questions. For example, scientists started measuring carbon in Earth's atmosphere in 1958. Over time, they gathered huge amounts

⚠ Companies that produce oil benefit when the public has doubts about climate change.

of data. This information helped show a clear link between carbon gases and global warming.

However, climate change deniers misuse skepticism. They use it to cast doubt on all climate science, even though many parts are supported by strong evidence. For groups such as fossil fuel companies, this doubt is useful. Fuel companies do not need everyone to believe that climate change is fake. If enough people have doubts, action is less likely. Without action, fossil fuel companies continue to profit.

# CHAPTER 6

# MAKING CONNECTIONS

Climate change is an incredibly complex issue. As a result, reporters cannot cover every aspect of climate change in a single article. The crisis affects life on Earth in many ways. However, reporters have focused on certain climate issues more than others. For example, polar bears have received huge amounts of attention. That's partly because the climate crisis threatens the bears' Arctic home. In addition, many people care about

**Climate change can lead to an increase in droughts, which can kill crops.**

polar bears. So, reporters often use them as a symbol of climate change.

The attention on polar bears has limits, however. First, climate change affects people as well as animals. **Indigenous** peoples have lived in the Arctic for thousands of years. By focusing on polar bears, reporters ignore Indigenous peoples. Also, most people don't live near the Arctic. For them, the heavy focus on polar bears can make climate change seem far away.

In response, some climate experts argue for more variety in reporting. For instance, they believe more local news stations should cover climate change. One program trains weather reporters. The program helps them connect local weather to climate change. That way, more viewers will understand that climate change is already happening where they live.

▲ By focusing on polar bears, reporters lead many people to believe climate change is a distant problem.

Climate change has wider impacts, too. For example, worsening floods and fires make it harder for crops to grow. Farmers lose money. Food prices go up. People may even run out of food. These results have negative impacts for businesses and for people's health. But the media is less likely to cover these impacts. As a result, people often don't understand that these issues are connected to the climate.

Many news sources also make it seem like people contribute to climate change equally.

However, that does not match the research. Between 1988 and 2017, more than 70 percent of all **greenhouse gas emissions** were created by just 100 companies. Wealthy people have contributed more to climate change than low-income people. Similarly, wealthy nations are a much larger cause of the crisis. That's because they have used more energy than lower-income nations.

Climate change also affects lower-income nations much more. These countries have fewer resources to respond to the crisis. Even in wealthy countries, the impacts of climate change are not felt equally. For instance, extreme weather harms low-income communities the most. These communities are often less protected from flooding. They are less able to afford the costs of leaving and rebuilding their homes.

▲ The climate crisis has already forced millions of people to leave their homes.

In the United States, climate change especially harms people of color. The impacts are most serious for Black and Indigenous peoples. That's partly because of **systemic racism**. Many parts of society are set up in a way that prevents people of color from accessing wealth.

However, these connections receive little coverage in the media. With less coverage, fewer people may understand the unequal impacts. As a result, low-income people and people of color continue to receive less support.

# CHANGE OR CRISIS?

The words the media uses to describe things matter. Sometimes news outlets make changes to the words they use. For instance, in 2019, the *Guardian* stopped using the phrase "climate change." Instead, it began using "climate crisis." The *Guardian* made this shift for a few reasons. One reason was that change can be good or bad. A change can also be large or small. And the change may not have a specific cause.

The problem with "change" came up at the 2020 US vice presidential debate. Vice President Mike Pence was asked about climate change. He answered, "The climate is changing. But the issue is, what's the cause? And what do we do about it?"[1] Pence's answer suggested that scientists did not yet know what was causing climate change. His words also suggested that action could wait.

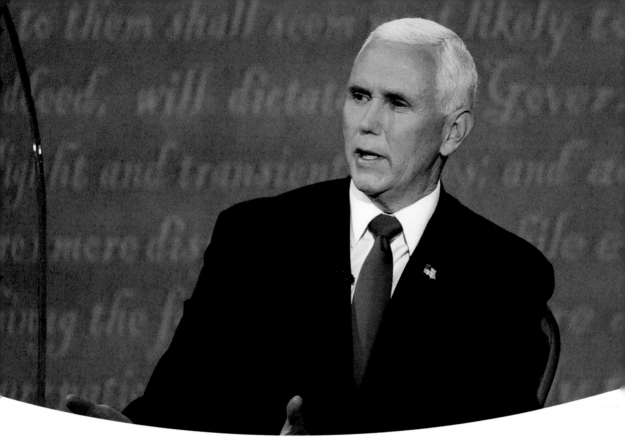

▲ In a 2020 debate, Vice President Mike Pence questioned the need for fast action on climate change.

In contrast, a "crisis" means the situation is serious. In a crisis, people need to act as soon as possible. The *Guardian*'s shift in wording drew attention to the serious nature of the problem. The shift also showed the need for quick action.

1. "Quotes from Policy-Heavy Debate Between Kamala Harris, Mike Pence." *Reuters*. Reuters, 7 Oct. 2020. Web. 5 Jan. 2021.

# CHAPTER 7

# SOLUTIONS

Coverage of climate change often focuses on the harm it can lead to. And these dangers are very real. Climate change is already causing problems around the world. If climate change gets worse, the risks of harm become worse, too. As a result, the media often focuses on the risks people face. This focus helps deliver important information. After all, people cannot act if they do not know about the problem.

**Rather than focusing on the solutions to climate change, many reporters discuss the problems it causes, such as storm damage.**

However, the media often spends less time on the solutions to climate change. Many climate experts believe news sources should highlight solutions more often. One key solution is to change energy sources. Solar and wind power can replace oil, coal, and gas. People can also replace older machines with more-efficient ones. Then, people will use less energy overall.

In addition, people can restore wetlands and forests. These regions help remove carbon gases from the air. Certain technologies can also remove carbon gases. And scientists are studying more ways to help. However, these solutions get little media attention compared to all the problems.

When news sources do discuss solutions to the climate crisis, they often show bias. For example, many reporters focus on how much climate action would cost. Some imply that these costs are

▲ By preserving and restoring forests, people can limit the amount of carbon in the atmosphere.

simply too great. It is true that climate solutions are expensive. However, economists have shown that these costs are far lower than the costs of letting climate change get worse.

Climate reporting often explains solutions in terms of sacrifices. These sacrifices include using less energy, flying less, and having fewer children. However, reports are less likely to describe how climate action may improve people's lives. For example, fossil fuel companies pollute the air and

⚠ Protesters demand that lawmakers take action to address the climate crisis.

water. So, shifting away from fossil fuels could increase the health of many people. This shift would especially help people of color, who are more likely to live in high-pollution areas. And many climate solutions could provide people with well-paying jobs.

Finally, reporting has tended to focus on **consumer** solutions to climate change. Some articles discuss what individuals should or should not buy. Others suggest that individuals make changes to reduce their personal climate impact. One example is not eating meat. These articles can place blame on individuals for climate change. They also imply that individuals' actions are the main way to help.

In truth, only large-scale solutions can solve the crisis. Governments and large companies must take action against climate change. Individual actions still matter, though. For instance, individuals can ask their governments to take action. They can also take part in protests. These gatherings show that many people care about the topic. They also help attract attention. Climate protests are taking place around the world. And the media is taking note. Reporting about the topic will likely continue to change.

# BIAS IN REPORTING ON CLIMATE CHANGE

*Write your answers on a separate piece of paper.*

**1.** Write a paragraph explaining the main ideas of Chapter 4.

**2.** Do you think the media should use the phrase "climate crisis" or "climate change"? Why?

**3.** Approximately what percent of scientists agree about human-caused climate change?

> **A.** 44 percent
> **B.** 71 percent
> **C.** 97 percent

**4.** Why might individual consumer choices be less helpful than actions such as protesting?

> **A.** Individual consumer choices always change a large company's actions.
> **B.** Protests can cause larger groups, such as governments and companies, to act.
> **C.** Consumer choices make no impact on climate change.

*Answer key on page 48.*

# GLOSSARY

**bias**
An attitude that causes someone to treat certain ideas unfairly.

**climate change**
A human-caused global crisis involving long-term changes in Earth's temperature and weather patterns.

**conservative**
Supporting traditional views or values, often resisting changes.

**consumer**
Having to do with buying goods and services.

**greenhouse effect**
When gases that absorb heat enter the atmosphere and increase the average temperature of a planet.

**greenhouse gas emissions**
Gases that are released into the atmosphere by factories, cars, and many other sources, contributing to global warming.

**Indigenous**
Native to a region, or belonging to ancestors who lived in a region before colonists arrived.

**Industrial Revolution**
Starting in Great Britain in the 1700s, a huge economic shift involving the use of powerful machines and mass production.

**progressives**
People who support changes to traditional views or values.

**systemic racism**
The legal, political, and economic systems that harm people of color.

# TO LEARN MORE

## BOOKS

Grant, John. *Debunk It! Fake News Edition: How to Stay Sane in a World of Misinformation*. Minneapolis: Lerner Publications, 2019.

Hand, Carol. *Climate Scientists*. Minneapolis: Abdo Publishing, 2020.

McPherson, Stephanie Sammartino. *Hothouse Earth: The Climate Crisis and the Importance of Carbon Neutrality*. Minneapolis: Lerner Publications, 2021.

## NOTE TO EDUCATORS

Visit **www.focusreaders.com** to find lesson plans, activities, links, and other resources related to this title.

# INDEX

Answer Key: 1. Answers will vary; 2. Answers will vary; 3. C; 4. B